THE
CONTEMPORARY
CONDITION

THE CONTEMPORARY CONDITION 06

Notes on the Type, Time, Letters & Spirits
Dexter Sinister

Published by Sternberg Press, 2017

Series edited by Geoff Cox & Jacob Lund

Published in partnership with ARoS Aarhus Art Museum
and The Contemporary Condition research project
at Aarhus University, made possible by a grant
from the Danish Council for Independent Research,
September 2015 – August 2018.

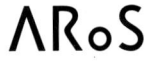

AARHUS ART MUSEUM DENMARK

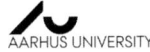

AARHUS UNIVERSITY

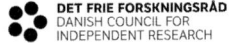

DET FRIE FORSKNINGSRÅD
DANISH COUNCIL FOR
INDEPENDENT RESEARCH

contemporaneity.au.dk

Design: Dexter Sinister
Printing and binding: BUD Potsdam
Paper: Cyclus Print

ISBN 978-3-95679-345-5

Sternberg Press
Caroline Schneider
Karl-Marx-Allee 78
D-10243 Berlin
www.sternberg-press.com

Notes on the Type, Time, Letters & Spirits

Dexter Sinister

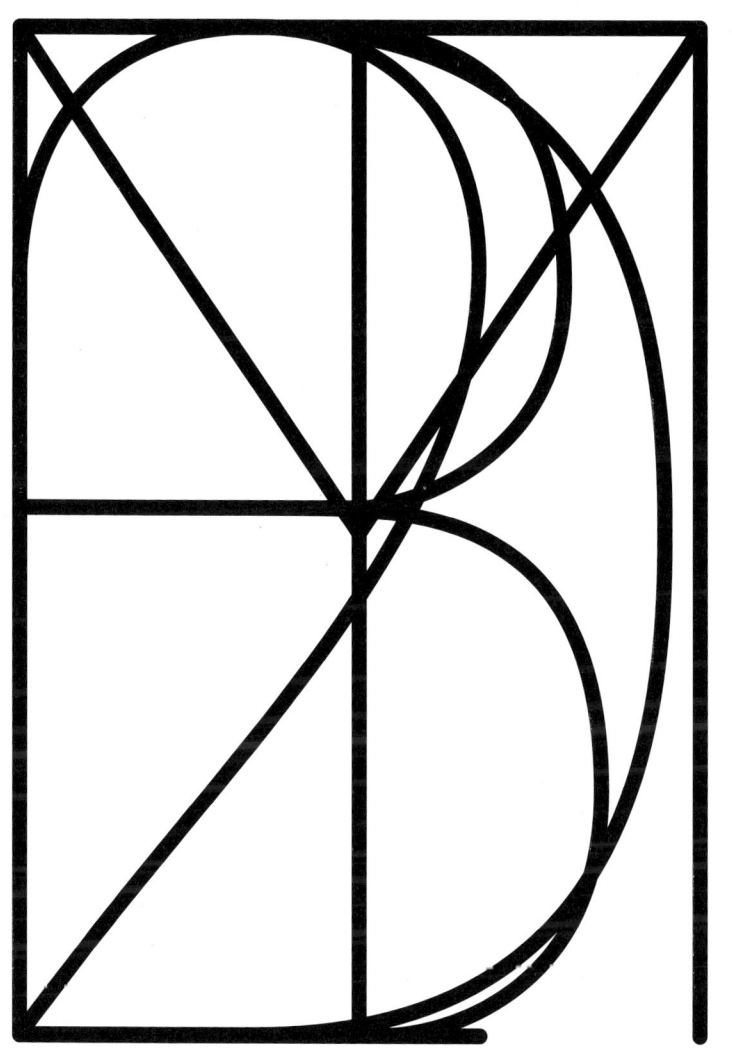

Previous page: MTDBT2F composite glyph

A Note on the Type

PEN = 0, 1, 1, 0, WEIGHT = 100, SLANT = 0, SUPER-
NESS = 0.75, CURLYNESS = 0:

This is Meta-the-difference-between-the-two-Font, a typeface
designed by Dexter Sinister in 2010, and derived using
MetaFont, the now-thirty-year-old computer typography
system programmed by Donald Knuth in 1979.

MetaFont is both a programming language and its own
interpreter, a swift trick where it first provides a vocabulary
and then decodes its syntax back to the native binary machine
language of 1s and 0s. Knuth originally intended MetaFont as
a helper application for TeX, the computer typesetting system
he created to facilitate high-quality typography directly by
authors. Donald Knuth, a Stanford professor and author of
the multivolume computer-science bible *The Art of Computer
Programming* (1971), was dismayed on receiving galley
proofs for the second edition of his book. The publisher had
just switched from traditional hot metal typesetting to a digital
system and the typographic quality was far worse than the
original 1971 edition. Knuth figured that setting letters on a
page was simply a matter of ink or no-ink, on or off, 1 or 0,
and therefore a perfect problem for the computer. He planned
on spending a six-month sabbatical writing a typesetting
program and produced (almost 10 years later) the near-
ubiquitous (in mathematics and science publishing, anyway)
computer typesetting program, TeX. MetaFont was designed
from the start as TeX's manual assistant and faithful servant,
producing as required the high-quality fonts at whatever size
and shape on command.

MetaFont was also intended as a tool for designing new
typefaces on its own. As MetaFont was programmed by Knuth,
a mathematician, the resulting typographic design method
relies on equations (multivariable algebra and a bit of vector
arithmetic) to specify letterforms and computer code to compile

these instructions into a usable font—all of which is more the native province of mathematicians than type designers.

In the American Mathematical Society's prestigious Josiah Willard Gibbs Lecture of July 4, 1978, Knuth gave a talk titled "Mathematical Typography," and suggested, "We may conclude that a mathematical approach to the design of alphabets does not eliminate the artists who have been doing the job for so many years." True enough, but the relatively steep technical slope of using MetaFont for type designers, combined with the limited interest in making typefaces by mathematicians, has resulted in only several handfuls of MetaFonts being produced over the last thirty years. As such, scant documentation and support exists for someone trying to create a MetaFont today.

OK, let's change the parameters of what you've been reading by setting the following excerpt from trader/philosopher Elie Ayache's essay, "In the Middle of the Middle of the Event" (2014) in Meta-the-difference-between-the-two-Font, with PEN = 1, 2, 10, 30, WEIGHT = 30, SLANT = 0.3, SUPERNESS = 0.7, CURLYNESS = 0. Like so:

I traded options for ten years, on the floor, both here in London and in Paris, so I have some direct knowledge of the market itself as a material and as a medium, and not a theory. On the other hand, I am an engineer by training, so I know a lot about probability theory, and after being a trader for ten years, for the next ten years of my career I created a company that specializes in pricing derivatives. It is a software company, and what we develop in the company relies very much on probability theory and on the "metaphysical framework" whereby, in order to model the unpredictable, first of all you have to identify the different scenarios that may take place. And, according to all of us here, this is the major weakness of probability theory and of the metaphysical thinking of possibility when confronted by the pure contingent event: in order to model something and to project it in thought, you have first of all to give yourself the list of scenarios and then simply assign probabilities to them. That's very easy when you are playing roulette or dice, because you know beforehand that the dice have six faces, so you know what the scenarios are; and in playing roulette, also in playing cards, you know what the scenarios are, so it's very easy then to agree or disagree with one another, whether we should put a 50% chance on the coin or not, whether it's wise or not — it becomes only a rather local and confined disagreement about what the probabilities are. But the main thing is that the scenarios are identified beforehand, and that's the major weakness.

I studied probability theory, and every day my company develops software based on it — and I can assure you, it's probability theory in its most sophisticated branches. We owe these sophisticated theories to finance; the mathematicians involved in probability theory and the like are all working in the field of finance, because it's not probability like dice. You have to know a lot about stochastic calculus and other very advanced things, about volatility ... These terms are perhaps more familiar to us now (!) but basically, volatility relates to the fact that if you have something that is MOVING, you have the trend of the price — an upward or downward trend — from which volatility measures the standard deviation: the noise of the thing as it follows its trend. So, volatility is the measure of risk; and today, indeed, we have models in finance that deal with the volatility of volatility, and with jumps. I mean to say that it's a very sophisticated field, and you have people who have PhDs, you have researchers, and you have *papers and books on probability theory and quantitative models.*

However, the philosophical foundations of this are very weak, because it hasn't changed at all. It relies on you beforehand having to model the possibilities. So the question is — and this is a question that Nassim Taleb, in his 2007 book The Black Swan *has asked in a very good way — what if we are really dealing with a CONTINGENT event, a pure contingent event of such a kind that, beforehand, we don't know what it's going to look like? When we don't know from which roulette wheel or from which dice the outcome will be drawn — that is what a major event really is. And that's what Nassim Taleb calls a "black swan," which he defines as an event that is very improbable. Now, of course it's improbable — but it's even worse than improbable. It wasn't even part of any list of scenarios that you had beforehand. So one of my criticisms of Nassim is to tell him that we shouldn't even call it improbable, because, if the event was not part of the pre-given list of possibilities, probability does not even apply to it.*

Unlike more common computer outline font formats such as TrueType or Postscript Type 1, a MetaFont font is constructed of strokes drawn with set-width pens. Instead of describing the outline of the character directly by drawing each letter shape inside and outside, counter and letterform, a MetaFont file describes only the basic pen path or skeleton letter. Perhaps better imagined as the ghost that comes in advance of a particular letterform, a MetaFont character is defined only by a set of equations rather than hard-coded coordinates and outline shapes. So it is then possible to treat parameters such as aspect ratio, slant, stroke width, serif size, (curlyness!?) and so on as abstracted input values that can change in each glyph definition, creating not a set of set letters, but instead a set of set parameters, any of which can be changed each time the font is rendered. By changing the value at one location in the MetaFont file, a consistent change is produced throughout the entire font. The resulting collection of glyph definitions and input parameters is not then a single font, but instead, a meta-font.

Let's try that again ... You may recall from earlier that MetaFont is both a language and its own interpreter. (What does that mean?) Taking a clue from that riddle, we could turn MetaFont's name back on itself by taking it apart, beginning with the end—"font."

"Font" is a word whose current common usage (particularly in the context of personal computers) has twisted its exact definition. Returning to its roots, a "font" is simply a collection of characters of one particular design or, precisely, typeface. More specifically a "font" is the particular realization of a certain typeface in a certain medium, according to certain parameters such as size, width, weight, style, contrast, and shape—for example, a font of William Caslon's letters cast in hot lead at 14 points, or a font of Standard Grotesque at 96 points carved from oak, or even a full font of 12 pixel letters stretched 150% and rendered on a 72-dpi screen from the Arial typeface. However, this collection of parameters (size, width, weight, etc.) according to which a font is rendered from a particular typeface are not fixed. New parameters can be added at will, and this is where the "Meta" of MetaFont begins.

"Meta-" is a prefix of Greek origin that originally simply meant "after," but due to a strange turn of events came to mean "of a higher order, beyond" in Latin and later modern languages (excluding Greek, where it retains its original meaning). Its current use is from Aristotle's book on metaphysics, but he would never have called it that. Aristotle would refer to the subject of that book as first philosophy or theology.

The title *Metaphysics* comes from Andronicus of Rhodes (1st century BC), who was the first editor of Aristotle and placed the book on metaphysics after the book on physics in his compilation (so, it was quite literally "after" physics).

So then you have metalanguages (languages used to describe languages), meta-history (the study of how people view and study history), meta-theorems (theorems about theorems), meta-rules (rules about rules), etc. Indeed, you can "meta" just about anything.

Let's try another version of MTDBT2F, demonstrated using a later excerpt from Ayache's text with PEN = 0, 1, 1, 0, WEIGHT = 0, SLANT = 0.0, SUPERNESS = 0.5, CURLYNESS = 0:

"Pierre Menard, Author of the Quixote" is a very short story by Jorge Luis Borges, where he tells the story of the life of a French writer called Pierre Menard, in the early 20th century, who has spent the last 20 years of his life writing two chapters of Cervantes' *Don Quixote*, writing them word by word. It's weird, because you tend to think, well, you're just copying them … But no, if you read Borges' story, you can trust Borges to convince you that, actually, Pierre Menard has done something original. When you read the story, you are actually convinced that he is producing an original work, the work of a creator, even, of an artist — yet he knows what he is doing. It's not even that he didn't know that Cervantes had already written *Don Quixote* — he knew that. He wanted, on purpose, to write *Don Quixote*. So, he is creating, he's producing something new, something contingent, let's say, something that could have been otherwise. After all, there is no creation if you're just copying *Don Quixote*. Yet the set of possibilities is limited to only one, because he knows beforehand that he is going to.actually write *Don Quixote*.

So, my question is, where do you place the creativity of Pierre Menard?

To my mind, it lies in that blank residuum that I'm pursuing; and that must be beyond possibilities, because in the space of possibilities, Pierre Menard is doing nothing. He is doing totally zero, because in the space of possibilities the work exists, it's *Don Quixote*, and he's just copying it. If you believe in the metaphysics of possibility and probability, where everything is framed in identified states of the world, and so on, then Pierre Menard is doing nothing, totally nothing. Yet by reading Borges, you are really led to believe it possible that Pierre Menard has done something original; and the key thing to me is that what Pierre Menard has done is to WRITE two chapters. He didn't read them, he didn't just think of them. So, he really NEEDED the MATERIAL MEDIUM, the writing itself, in order to produce something that, when you read it, you say, well, although it's the same — it has the same identity as Cervantes' novel — it is materially a new work. And although my main object is the markets and finance, although that's important, and I identify the medium of contingency as the market in my specific case, in the end its generalization is also writing.

I also happen to be a writer, so I also speak for myself: writing, to me, is something that is beyond probability and "states of the world." It's something where the writer can really throw himself into a process of writing, blindly so to speak — and one of my favorite expressions is that he is then *traversed by contingency,* so he almost surprises himself with what he is writing. To me, that's writing: even though you may have thought about it, and you had planned it, there are thoughts that you can only have through writing. I'm sure everyone has found that: there is no use really in planning in advance what you are going to write. Even if you do that, chances are that you'll end up writing something different. I think that the true spark of writing comes when you find yourself surprised by what you have written; and I would even claim that there are thoughts that you can only have through the material process of writing.

So, writing to me is an attempt to try to get to that extraordinary or residual thing that surpasses probability and the states of the usual metaphysical conception; and which would allow us to TWIST chronology in such a way that, even though the event happens and it is only after the event that we can think it, somehow we establish communication with it outside time. Remember, I need to twist time itself in order to be able to predict the event "beforehand," even though it has happened.

In 2009, the *New Yorker* ran "The Unfinished," a piece about American writer David Foster Wallace following his death six months earlier. Midway through the tribute, D. T. Max quotes from an early letter that Wallace sent to Gerald Howard of Penguin Books, in which he explains that his work is neither primarily "realism" nor "metafiction," but rather, "if it's anything, it's meta-the-difference-between-the-two."

Typically, it's a throwaway line that returns, then stays with you. Does the "difference" here refer to a mathematical distinction in quantity, or to a more common sense of distinction or dissimilarity (or even disagreement)? Or both? Wallace's chain-of-words is as slippery as the logically recursive sentence "The first rule is: there are no rules," but with a difference. Instead of simply setting up an endless loop between two poles, it observes that loop from a higher point of concentrated disinterest. There's no simple way out of this one, and yet there seems to be just enough there to keep trying.

Zadie Smith makes a case for this in an essay on Wallace, using his short story "The Depressed Person" from *Brief*

Interviews with Hideous Men as arch example: "The effect on the reader is powerful, unpleasant. Quite apart from being forced to share one's own mental space with the depressed person's infinitely dismal consciousness, to read those spiral sentences is to experience that dread of circularity embedded in the old joke about recursion (to understand recursion you must first understand recursion)."

Exporting Wallace's chain from literature to a more general use, we could plug other values into the equation. For "realism" we could insert "practice" and for "metafiction" perhaps "theory." (These poles can be endlessly swapped with similarly productive confusion — try "concrete"/"abstract" or "modernism"/"postmodernism.") And yet the "meta-the-difference-between-the-two" between any of these two isn't simply resolved by some alchemical fusion, as in "practice" + "theory" = "praxis," practice informed by theory and vice versa. Less of a compound than an extraction, more a subtraction than an addition, MTDBT2 is then actually a skeleton, a script, or a good idea in advance of its realization.

Donald Knuth began his Josiah Gibbs Lecture, "Mathematical Typography" with an apology of sorts, saying, "I will be speaking today about work in progress, instead of completed research; this was not my original intention when I chose the subject of this lecture, but the fact is I couldn't get my computer programs working in time." And he continues, "Fortunately it is just as well that I don't have a finished product to describe to you today, because research in mathematics is generally much more interesting while you're doing it than after it's all done."

Meta-the-difference-between-the-two-Font has a similarly incomplete character. As a set of simple letterforms and a collection of meta-design parameters, MTDBT2F will create unending numbers of different fonts from now onwards, always only moving forward and compiling a collection of surface effects onto its essential skeleton to produce a growing family of "hollow" fonts whose forms have more in common with handwriting than they do with hot metal counterpunches (not to mention modern digital fonts). The clumsy result, with its chewy name Meta-the-difference-between-the-two-Font, arrives before the effect that is applied to it, returning to a moment before fonts, just before Gutenberg's first black-letter Gothic types attempted to match the scribe's penmanship. At this point, to computer-automate the production of hand-written calligraphy, and to more or less ignore 400 years of typographic tradition, is essentially absurd.

It seemed like a good idea at the time.

So here's one last trial with a third and final excerpt from Ayache's essay repurposed once more as dummy text, with the parameters now set to PEN = 0, 1, 1, 0, WEIGHT = 130, SLANT = -0.1, SUPERNESS = 0.7, CURLYNESS = 0:

This thought must be resisted. We have to suppress possibility in our thinking of the contingency of the actual world in exactly the same way as we did in our thinking of the future contingent world. We have to recognize the actual world to be contingent without identifying alternative possible worlds that are supposed to have made it so. Those possible worlds are only a fiction. We should recognize the contingency of the actual world through the one and only reality of its contingency, not the unreality (or fiction) of its possible variations.

This is just saying that the present actual world, which — as we all agree — is every bit as contingent as the future world, actually does not dwell in a well-identified state, either. Sure enough, it is present and it is actual. But with what authority do we partition it into recognizable events and states of affairs, and decide what is an event and what is not? Once you radically drop the identification of states (either actual or possible), time becomes incidental, really. There should really be no difference between the present world and the future world, except the incidental fact that the one succeeds to the other in time. In terms of what truly matters here, namely contingency, the present world and the future world are equal. This also means they are equal in terms of reality, which is the other side of contingency (as contingency is the only thing that is real). "Succession is not an illusion; it is only that succession is the shallowest thing," writes French philosopher François Zourabichvili.

The future event is real; it is here alright; yet it does not exist yet. It is only the course of time that will make it exist and will actualize it. But time is incidental to the event — time is not the only way we should relate to the future event. What if the future contingent event had a PLACE instead of a time or a timing, a place we could inhabit independently of time? What if the identification of the event — which can only happen in (due) time — were not what truly mattered in the event? What if the actuality of the event were only one side of its reality — an accidental side, that is, which only depends on accidental time — and the more essential aspect, or trait, or stroke, or characteristic of the reality of the event were its bare contingency? What if we managed to relate to its essential trait and contingency without relating to IT as an identified occurrence? Since we relate to its trait outside time, through this special medium of contingency that remains to be discovered, and no longer necessarily relate to it as an identified occurrence, can we still be said to predict it? Is it even important to PREDICT it? Perhaps a more essential relation can be established with it — a "work relation" instead of a "state relation." That we should work our way through that special medium of contingency instead of expecting or predicting the event in time may be the best way to deal with the event and to "predict" it somehow.

It may be wrong to expect the true contingent event
in time or in possibility. It may even be wrong to expect
it at all because it is truly unpredictable and unexpectable.
In Badiou, we seem fascinated by the fact that the
event emerges out of nothing and we wonder how this
is possible. We place ourselves in time, before the event,
and we wonder what could have preceded the event,
in time, so to announce it. I say forget about time.
Go from the reality of the contingent world that will be
actualized in the future and step back to the present spot
while remaining caught in reality (that is, while
avoiding stepping into the tree of possibility). This sounds
impossible, literally, because we seem unable to step
back in time without awakening possibility.

Note: The Elie Ayache excerpts are
drawn from "In the Middle of the Middle
of the Event," *Bulletins of The Serving
Library* #8 (2015), itself a re-worked
version of "In the Middle of the Event,"
originally published in *The Medium
of Contingency* (London: Ridinghouse;
Falmouth: Urbanomic, 2011).

```
** initialization complete. **\r
Welcome to Meta-the-Difference-Between-the-Two-Font.
Today is Fri Mar  2 15:27:30 EST 2012
*
Current working directory is /Users/reinfurt/Documents/Projects/META THE DIFFERE
NCE BETWEEN THE 2 FONT/Source/Meta-the-difference between-the-two-Font/v0.6c
```

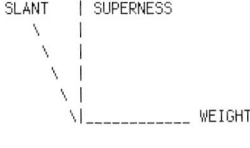

```
                    PEN ===>

WEIGHT=50.0000000000000000000
SLANT=.2000000000000000000
SUPER=.5750000000000000000
PENTYPE=0
PENX=349.50000000000000000000
PENY=100
PENR=216.0000000000000000000
Welcome to Meta-the-Difference-Between-the-Two-Font.
Today is Fri Mar  2 15:27:30 EST 2012
*
Current working directory is /Users/reinfurt/Documents/Projects/META THE DIFFERE
NCE BETWEEN THE 2 FONT/Source/Meta-the-difference between-the-two-Font/v0.6c
mftrace 1.2.16
Font `mtdbt2f4d'...
Using encoding file: `/usr/local/texlive/2011basic/texmf/fonts/enc/dvips/tetex/m
tdbt2f.enc'
Running Metafont...
Tracing bitmaps... [0][1][2][3][4][5][6][7][8][9][10][11][12][13][14][15][16][17
][18][19][20][21][22][23][24][25][26][27][28][29][30][31][32][33][34][35][36][37
][38][39][40][41][42][43][44][45][46][47][48][49][50][51][52][53][54][55][56][57
][58][59][60][61][62][63][64][65][66][67][68][69][70][71][72][73][74][75][76][77
][78][79][80][81][82][83][84][85][86][87][88][89][90][91][92][93][94][95][96][97
][98][99][100][101][102][103][104][105][106][107][108][109][110][111][112][113][
114][115][116][117][118][119][120][121][122][123][124][125][126][127][129][130][
131][132][134][135][136][137][138][140][141][142][143]
Assembling raw font to `mtdbt2f4d.pfa.raw'...
Copyright (c) 2000-2011 by George Williams.
 Executable based on sources from 13:48 GMT 22-Feb-2011-D.
 Library based on sources from 13:48 GMT 22-Feb-2011.
** metafont ok **
** fontforge ok **
** mtdbt2f ok **
Bye.
** mtdbt2f-make ok **
Bye.
** sleep for 0 seconds **
```

Letter & Spirit

In the early 1980s, on the pages of academic design journal *Visible Language*, a classic thesis-antithesis-synthesis played out around the technological and philosophical fine points of computer-assisted type design. Stanford professor Donald Knuth begins with his article, "The Concept of a Meta-font" (Winter 1981). Two years prior, Knuth had conceived and programmed MetaFont—a software that enabled users to generate unlimited numbers of fonts by controlling a limited set of parameters. The article is a performative account of his intervening attempts, using MetaFont to harness the essential "intelligence" of letterforms. In Knuth's view, the way a single letter is drawn—an *a priori* A, say—presupposes and informs all other letters in the same font. This information can be isolated, turned into a set of instructions, and put to work computer-automating the generation of new characters by filling in the features between two or more variables such as weight or slant.

Such intelligence is (and has always been) implicit in any typeface, but Knuth is out to omit all ambiguity and install a more definite system. He acknowledges that this preoccupation with designing meta-level instructions rather than the fonts themselves is typical of the contemporary inclination to view things "from the outside, at a more abstract level, with what we feel is a more mature understanding." From this elevated vantage, MetaFont was set up to oversee "how the letters would change in different circumstances."

A year later, fellow mathematician Douglas Hofstadter responded with his "MetaFont, Metamathematics, and Meta-physics" (Autumn 1982). While "charmed" by Knuth's thesis, and admitting the bias of his own interests in artificial intelligence and aesthetic theory, Hofstadter proceeds to shoot down his colleague's apparent claim that the shape of any given letterform is "mathematically containable." To support his case, he invokes mathematician Kurt Gödel's incompleteness theorems, which assert that any account of a logically coherent system always contains one root-level instance that cannot itself be contained by that account. Hofstadter's antithesis then usefully couches the debate in terms of "the letter of the law" versus "the spirit of the law," a familiar antinomy that posits an absolute deference to a set of set rules against a consistent yet fluid set of principles. Our prevailing legal system is, of course, based on both: judges base their decisions on firmly established precedent, but also map uncharted territory by bringing the full range of their experience to bear on specific cases "in a remarkably fluid way." In this manner, the law itself adapts.

Hofstadter argues that an accordingly *spirited* conception of type design would therefore renounce Knuth's ur-A-FORM in favor of a yet-higher-level abstraction, an ur-A-ESSENCE; the fundamental difference being that Hofstadter's notion of "intelligence" extends beyond a Platonic shape, allowing for the concept of *what constitutes an A* to change too—beyond what we can reasonably conceive of this possibly being in the future. Each new instance of an A adds to our general understanding of this idea (and ideal), which is necessarily assembled backwards over time.

Hofstadter includes this illustration of two letters vying for the same "typographic niche," to make himself clear:

Neatly enough, the following year a linguistics professor called Geoffrey Sampson drafted a brief response to Hofstadter's response to Knuth, titled "Is Roman Type an Open-Ended Question?" (Autumn 1983), which, it turns out, is decidedly rhetorical. Sampson argues that Hofstadter's hairsplitting unfairly and unnecessarily exaggerates Knuth's claims to the point of warping both his meaning and intentions. There is enough metaphysical latitude, the linguist referees, to accommodate both points of view without recourse to the misery of analytical one-upmanship. Sampson's synthesis of letter and spirit contends that it is perfectly reasonable to conceive of letterforms as both a closed system (Knuth's A-shape) AND as an open-ended system (Hofstadter's A-ness). Relatively speaking, it depends *what you're after.*

The history of typography is marked by a persistent drive to rationalize. Following the invention of movable type in the mid-15th century, the Renaissance saw several attempts to prescribe the construction of the Roman alphabet: Fra Luca Pacioli's alphabet of perfect relations, Albrecht Dürer's letters of mathematical instructions, and Geoffroy Tory's humanistic rationalizations. These attempts were, however, essentially calligraphic exercises in determining "divine proportions": the first to apply Enlightenment rationality to properly technical ends was the so-called Romain du Roi, or the "King's Roman." Commissioned by Louis XIV in Paris at the end of the 17th century, it was a typical Age of Reason project—the imposition of a mathematically rigorous structure on forms that had, until now, developed organically, initially shaped by the human hand (calligraphy, inscriptions, woodcuts) and adapted according to the various demands and opportunities of the printing press and its attendant technologies. Designed by "a royal committee of philosophers and technologists" from the Academy of Sciences, the Romain du Roi was initially plotted on an orthogonal 48 × 48 grid,

and a corollary "sloped Roman" italic variant derived by
skewing the upright version.

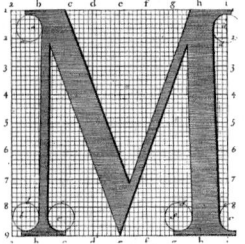

The coordinates were first engraved as a set of instructions,
then cut into punches to make metal type, which were to be
used exclusively on official or state-approved materials. In this
way, the king's letters exerted state power like a great seal
or particular signature.

Such ratiocination was revived at the Bauhaus in the
1920s, in line with two of the school's foundational principles
set up to meet the demands of industrialization: the omission
of ornament and the reduction to geometric elements. The
most celebrated outcome was Herbert Bayer's 1925 Universal
Alphabet, a pared-down sans-serif comprised exclusively of
lowercase characters. Bayer adapted the basic glyphs for
typewriter and handwriting, experimented with phonetic
alternatives, and proposed a wide family of variants, such
as the condensed bold version drawn on this panel:

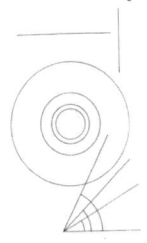

Alongside the basic character set (minus a presumably redundant *o*, but with alternatives to *a* and *g*, as well as two *d*s that anticipate lighter weights), Bayer has further abstracted the tools he used to draw it: ruler, T-square, set square, compass, and protractor. As such, the drawing captions itself, pointing to its point — that this is a project *intrinsically concerned with a particular mode of construction.*

Around the same time, fellow Bauhausler Josef Albers followed similar principles to slightly different ends with his Stencil Alphabet. This, too, was a single-case font, now entirely configured from ten rudimentary shapes, also typically isolated and presented alongside the assembled letters. Drawn and photographed for exclusive use in the school's own publications and publicity, these elemental Bauhaus fonts remained closeted explorations rather than properly industrial products. Neither was developed into a "working" typeface, mass-manufactured in metal for wider use. Outside the school, though, prominent *Werkbunder* Paul Renner toned down the hard geometry with gentler, "humanist" sensibilities — more modulation, less harsh on the eye — to yield his commercially successful Futura. When it was issued in 1927, godfather of the nascent "New Typography," Jan Tschichold, wrote that

> it cannot be open to one person to create the letterform of our age, which is something that must be free of personal traces. It will be the work of several people, among whom one will probably find an engineer.

During the 1930s, British type designer Stanley Morison was in charge of Monotype, the most significant type foundry of the day. Morison was solicited by the *Times*, London's principal newspaper, to take out a £1,000 full-page advert. Morison responded yes, as long he could typeset the page himself, because the newspaper's existing design was in such a dire state. This conversation reportedly carried itself up the *Times*' chain of command, prompting its director to invite Morison to oversee a complete overhaul of the paper's typography. Morison accepted, again on one condition — that the paper abolish the use of full points after isolated proper nouns, which he (rightly) considered superfluous and an example of the sort of typographic depravity he intended to stamp out. The paper removed the offending punctuation, and Morison climbed aboard.

Newspaper typography is a particularly sensitive art. Minute adjustments have critical knock-on effects for the amount of news that can be issued — especially when multiplied by the massive circulation figures of the *Times*. In a 25-page memorandum, Morison concluded that the house typeface needed to be updated. What became Times New Roman, however, was neither redrawn from scratch nor merely an amendment of the existing version, but rather *amalgamated* from a number of different typefaces made at various points over the previous 400 years. The mongrel result was effectively collaged from past forms, so the lowercase *e* doesn't exactly "match" the lowercase *a* — at least not according to the usual standards of typographic consistency. Up close, Times New Roman is full of such quirks.

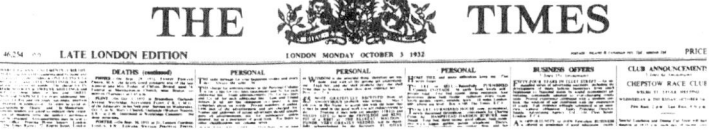

The design of letterforms usually manifests an individual designer's aesthetic impulse at a given point in time, but Times New Roman was the bastard offspring of MANY designers working ACROSS time, with Morison's role something like that of producer, editor, or arranger. The most frequently repeated account of the type's development suggests that Morison gave an existing type sample and some rough sketches to an assistant in the paper's advertising department, who duly cobbled together the new font. Whatever the story, in a note on HIS type, Morison concluded, auspiciously enough: "Ordinary readers, for whom a type is what it does, will be pleased to leave them to analyze the spirit of the letter."

French type designer Adrian Frutiger took the rational mapping of the Romain du Roi to another plateau with Univers, released by the foundry Deberny & Peignot in 1957. In line with the all-encompassing aspirations of mid-20th century Swiss design—locus of the so-called International Style— Univers was conceived as an unusually extended family of fonts. The standard palette of variants, traditionally limited to regular, italic, bold, and sometimes bold italic, was expanded sevenfold, yielding a total of 21 fonts to be cut at any given size. In the foundry's publicity, the family was usually housed in a two-dimensional matrix: an X-axis charts relative WIDTH interspersed with POSITION (Frutiger's term for slant), while the Y-axis charts relative WEIGHT. The family DNA is manifest in a few eccentricities, such as a square dot over the i and a double-barred lowercase a, while individual character sets are named according to their position in the matrix—55 for standard roman, 56 for standard oblique, 65 for medium roman, 66 for medium oblique, and so on.

Univers' matrix implies that the family could potentially procreate in any direction *ad infinitum*, and, in fact, the project has remained notably open since its inception. Frutiger himself reworked the typeface for digital release by Linotype in 1997, raising the total number of distinct character sets from the original 21 to 63. These included additions to both ends of the chart (Ultra Light and Extended Heavy), along with new monospace variants, requiring a third number to be added to the identifying code. In the wake of Univers' popularity, further dimensions have since been introduced, including extended character sets such as Central European, and non-Latin alphabets such as Greek, Cyrillic, Arabic, and Japanese. This globalization culminated in 2011 with Linotype rechristening the entire design "Univers Next."

Towards the end of "The Concept of a Meta-font," an admirably candid Knuth wonders: "The idea of a meta-font should now be clear. But what good is it?"

Hofstadter, for one, had an idea: "Never has an author had anything remotely like this power to control the final appearance of his or her work." Indeed, seeing his own writing in print years earlier, Knuth had been so upset by the shoddy standards of early digital typesetting that he resolved to do it himself—not unlike Morison with his *Times* advert. It took longer than expected, but a decade later, Knuth had designed TeX, an automated typesetting system still in wide use today within academic publishing. MetaFont was initally developed as handmaiden to TeX, to generate the fonts to be used within the broader tasks of document markup and page assembly. However, as MetaFont developed as a project in its own right, its purpose was less immediately apparent. At least by the time of his *Visible Language* article, MetaFont appears to be more a case of hobbyist tinkering in search of an eventual application.

To be fair, Knuth does propose a few uses, all of which were already possible but certainly enhanced by the speed of computer processing. One is the ability to adjust the details of a particular font in line with the limits of a given output device—to make letters thinner or less intricate, for instance, so as to resist type "filling in" with either ink (on paper) or pixels (on low-resolution monitors). A second is the possibility of generating countless iterations of the same basic design with slight differences in order to compare and contrast. But a more surprising (and most emphatically stated) third function of MetaFont, according to its creator, is to meet the "real need" of "mankind's need for variety." In other words, to create difference for the sake of difference.

And so the notion of developing MetaFont as an autonomous project rather than as one of TeX's machine parts appears to aim foremost at expanding the possibilities of literary expression—anticipating "greater freedom," a "typeface of one's own," "multiple fonts to articulate multiple voices," and so on. It's worth recalling, though, that when Knuth invented TeX in order to better typeset his own pages, or Morison refurbished the *Times*, their impetus was fundamentally reactive, not constructive. They weren't out to expand the possibilities for expression per se, only to reinstate standards that had been eroded—ones that had been established in the first place to articulate written language as clearly as possible, not to pile on the effects. As Knuth himself states, typefaces are more medium than message, to the extent that "A font should be sublime in its appearance but subliminal in its effect." What he didn't foresee (or at least worry over) is that mankind's real need for variety would tend towards the wholesale takeover of novelty as an end in itself.

In his 1928 book *One-Way Street*, the German cultural critic Walter Benjamin had already anticipated Knuth's "power to control the final appearance of his or her work," alluding to the artistic ends that an increased intimacy between writer and technology might foster. Specifically, he predicted that the writer will start to compose his work with a typewriter instead of a pen when "the precision of typographic forms has entered directly into the conception of his books," to the degree that "new systems with more variable typefaces might then be needed."

By writing directly into a mechanical form rather than a manuscript (as we're doing right now) the writer would be working closer to the nature of the multiplied result, and through an increasing awareness and gradual mastery of the form's new limitations and possibilities *the writing itself would evolve*; the shorter the distance between the raw material of words and their processed output, the more entwined the content and form from the outset. This line of thinking was more famously expounded by Benjamin in his 1936 essay "The Work of Art in the Age of Mechanical Reproduction," which more broadly argues that an authentic, pertinent art is the result of engagement with the latest technological innovations.

Benjamin was an active Marxist, committed to the notion that the technologies of manufacture—the "means of production"—ought to be owned by the people who operate them. In 1934's "The Author as Producer," instead of focusing on factories and workers, he attempts to pinpoint the nature of a *socially committed art.* Writing and the other arts, he writes, are grounded in social structures such as educational institutions and publishing networks, but rather than merely asking how an artist's work stands in relation TO these structures, he queries how it stands IN them. He demands that artists refrain from merely adopting political "content," propagating an ideological cause, and work instead to transform the root-level MEANS by which their work is produced and distributed. This "progressive" artistic approach INEVITABLY manifests a "correct" political tendency. The work practices in lieu of preaching.

Benjamin's first case study in "The Author as Producer" is the Soviet writer Sergei Tretyakov, who lived and worked on an agricultural commune for extended periods before writing his experiences up into a novel. He is offered as an exemplary "operative writer," implicating himself in the matter at hand, as opposed to the common hack who merely observes and "gives information." Benjamin's Exhibit A, though, is his immediate contemporary Bertolt Brecht, who subverted orthodox drama by way of his epic theatre's celebrated "distancing effects"—leaving the lights on, renouncing expository narrative, presenting a series of objective "situations" in order that the spectators draw their own conclusions. Via these and other manipulations of "technique," Brecht transformed "the functional relation between the stage and the public, text and production, director and actor."

Necessarily leading by his own and others' example, then, Benjamin urges the artist to perpetually reconsider his role away from prevailing norms, job descriptions, professional standards, and outside expectations generally. What MIGHT the work of a constructively minded "writer" constitute? Are the abilities to distill an opinion and turn a phrase adequately deployed via the regular mediums—newspaper columns, books, journals, and pamphlets—or might they be more usefully channeled through writing, say, captions to photographs, or scripts to make films, or indeed by renouncing writing altogether and taking up photography instead? Hence the essay's title is also its proposition: the writer (or artist) should be less a hemmed-in author than a free-ranging producer, closing the divide between her "intellectual" and "productive" activities.

In "A Note on the Type" (2010) we previously offered a history and extension of Knuth's MetaFont project. Our appreciative "note" (more a love letter written 30 years late) was then typeset in our own updated version of MetaFont—basically Knuth's project rebooted for the PostScript generation and, following a throwaway remark by the late David Foster

Wallace, rechristened Meta-the-difference-between-the-two-Font. That "single" note has since been published in multiple contexts and formats—on screens, pages, and walls. While all conform to the same basic essay template, each new instance adds three bits of writing by other people, each typeset in unique, freshly generated MTDBT2-fonts to demonstrate the software's essential plasticity. These extra texts have alluded to various facets of the project—repetition, habit, or the grey area between art and design, for example—that have suggested themselves as it has rolled palimpsestuously along.

Meta-the-difference-between-the-two-Font picked up where Knuth's MetaFont left off. In fact, the only OSTENSIBLE difference between the two is that the new version was re-scripted in contemporary code to run on current computers. When typefaces are reduced to on/off bits of information, the typographic norms established by metal type (and carried over into photocomposition) are no longer bound to material necessity—they can be ignored and modified, and this is precisely what Knuth did. However, it was only with the advent and proliferation of PostScript in the early 1980s that typefaces became "device independent," freed from their association with particular composing machines and their controlling companies. But beyond this nominal "language difference," MTDBT2F remained more or less faithful to MetaFont's founding principles—not least its wacko parameters borrowed from Knuth's Computer Modern font, which include SUPERNESS, CURLYNESS, and so on.

The ACTUAL difference between the two, on the other hand, is less easy to discern. One clue is the simple difference in time: what it meant to make it *then,* and what it means to make it *now.*

In his essay "On the New" (2002), philosopher and art theorist Boris Groys wrote:

Being new is, in fact, often understood as a combination of being different and being recently-produced. We call a car a NEW car if this car is different from other cars, and at the same time the latest, most recent model produced…. But as Kierkegaard pointed out, to be new is by no means the same as being different… the new is a DIFFERENCE WITHOUT DIFFERENCE, or a difference which we are unable to recognize because it is not related to any pre-given structural code.

He continues:

For Kierkegaard, therefore, the only medium for a possible emergence of the new is the ordinary, the "non-different," the identical—not the OTHER, but the SAME.

MTDBT2F is, more or less, the same as MetaFont, abiding the obvious fact that it swallows its predecessor. Although the result may look the same, it clearly can't be, because in addition to the "productive" software, the new version embeds its "intellectual" backstory—a story which is not merely supplementary but absolutely essential. MTDBT2F is a tool to generate countless PostScript fonts, sure, but it is *at least equally* a tool to think around and about MetaFont.

This broader notion is already ingrained in that original *Visible Language* debate, again most keenly foreseen by Hofstadter, who wrote that one of the best things MetaFont might do is inspire readers to chase after the intelligence of an alphabet, and "yield new insights into the elusive 'spirits' that flit about so tantalizingly, hidden just behind those lovely shapes we call 'letters.'" Hofstadter is still referencing fonts and computers here, but his sentiments can easily be read under what art critic Dieter Roelstraete recently called "the taunting of thought." In fact, Walter Benjamin closed "The Author as Producer" with the following summary:

You may have noticed that the chain of thought whose
conclusion we are approaching only presents the writer
with a single demand, the demand of REFLECTING,
of thinking about his position in the process of production.

At least as much as MTDBT2F serves as a functioning
typeface, or set of typefaces, then, it is also a red herring,
a carrot, and a mirror. It is a nominal setup for a nominal
subject to play out, typically moving in and out of focus, veering
off into other fields, and trespassing on other topics. In this
unruly manner, the font serves us (or anyone else) exactly as
it serves language—as rubber cement, a bonding agent.

In "The Designer as Producer," a quick riff on "The Author
as Producer" from 2004, design critic Ellen Lupton writes
that Benjamin "celebrated the proletarian ring of the word
'production,' and the word carries those connotations into
the current period," offering us "a new crack at materialism,
a chance to reengage the physical aspects of our work."
To claim, or reclaim, the "tools of production" in the arts today,
though, shouldn't imply some form of engagement, or worse,
RE-engagement, with heavy machinery, hand tools, hard
materials, or the studio (the art equivalent of the factory
floor). More plausibly, it implies digital code.
    Code resides in "the Hollows," the curiously named engine
room of immaterial media, domain of scripts and programs,
that has been likened by design group Metahaven to the stock
market crash: "surface without surface, the exposure of the
naked infrastructure or root level system language which
precedes surface itself, surface without its effects."
    Another recent essay titled after Benjamin and written
by Boris Groys, "Religion in the Age of Digital Reproduction,"
invokes the protagonists of *The Matrix* as being uniquely
equipped to perceive the workings of the Hollows. While Neo
& Co. were able to read image files as code, the average

spectator "does not have the magic pill ... that would allow him or her to enter the invisible digital space otherwise concealed behind the digital image." And auspiciously enough, Groys also draws on our now-familiar terms, letter and spirit.

In updating Benjamin's title, Groys signals the same basic investigation—of an existing phenomenon (this time religion rather than art) in a new milieu (digital rather than mechanical). Religious practice, he writes, has always involved the reproduction of institutionalized forms, but as Western religion has become increasingly personal and privatized, an unconditional "freedom of faith" has developed alongside traditional, conditional forms. Contemporary fundamentalist religion remains, by definition, grounded in the devout repetition of a fixed "letter" rather than a free "spirit"—material and external rather than essential and implied. This antinomy of "dead letter vs. living spirit" (which tallies easily enough with the legal one related by Hofstadter) informs all Western discourse on religion. On one hand, the typically "spirited" anti-fundamentalist account favors a living, powerful tradition capable of adapting its central message to different times and places, thus maintaining its vitality and relevance. Conversely, the ritualized repetition of the fundamentalist "letter" amounts to a kind of revolutionary stasis or violent rupture in the ever-changing order of things. Religious fundamentalism can thus be conceived as religion *after the death of the spirit*: letter and spirit are separated and polarized to the extent that the former no longer guarantees the latter. "A material difference is now JUST a difference," Groys writes. "There is no essence, no being, and no meaning underlying such a formal difference at a deeper level."

While earlier media suited and so precipitated the circulation of conditional religion (1:1 mechanically reproduced texts and images disseminated via orthodox channels), contemporary web-based media more closely approximate and so facilitate the unconditional—the wild dissemination of idiosyncratic views. And as digital reproduction supplants mechanical reproduction, the video image becomes the medium of choice. The cheap, anonymous, promiscuous character of digital information guarantees reproduction and dissemination more than any other historical medium. But what's REALLY being duplicated is, of course, the image's code—its invisible DNA.

In the 1930s, Benjamin had reasonably assumed that future technologies would only continue to guarantee the resemblance between an original and its copy, but now the opposite is true: each manifestation of the original is actually *different,* because typically overridden and recalibrated according to each spectator's local preferences (resolution, color calibration, style sheets, etc.), while ONLY THE CODE REMAINS THE SAME. In Groys's final analysis, spirit and letter are transposed from a metaphysical to a technological plane, where "spirit" is script, and each new visualization of that script is a corresponding "letter." (Picture m4vs, jpegs and mp3s as angels "transmitting their divine command.")

By now the terms are confused to the point of inversion: the so-called spirit of digital code is fixed, while the so-called letter of its various manifestations is fluid. Consequently, forms—surfaces—are no longer tethered to definite meaning, no longer plausible, and so no longer to be trusted.

This is old news. However, as digital media become increasingly ubiquitous, templates increasingly homogeneous and entrenched, the most likely place a "writer" might usefully "produce" today is in the Hollows. Hidden or invisible, and otherwise inaccessible to most, this is where we might conceivably reconnect spirit and letter, essence and identity, for "ordinary readers, for whom a type is what it does."

. . .

How to keep things moving?

MetaFont and MTDBT2F were both set up to generate an infinite number of individual typefaces by tweaking a few simple parameters at different points in time. But what if we make one of those parameters *time* itself?

First let's transpose the extant ones onto a 3-D graph, running WEIGHT (a kind of bold) along the X-axis, SLANT (more or less italic) up the Y, and extending SUPERNESS (a kind of chutzpah) off into the Z beyond. We'll ignore CURLYNESS for the time being, but we do have to account for a fourth factor, PEN, best conceived as a digital "nib" that determines the line's fundamental shape and angle at any given point.

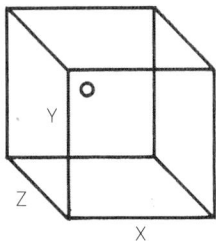

Now let's send that point *constantly moving* through this imaginary cube. As it wanders randomly and aimlessly through the space, it trails a script that renders an alphabet whose form morphs according to its position relative to the other parameters—not forgetting the fact that the point/nib/pen itself is in perpetual flux. And, crucially, it never stops. The outcome might be usefully apprehended as the potentially endless matrix of Frutiger's Univers, amalgamated over time like Morison's Times New Roman, articulating itself in the manner of Bayer's Geometric Alphabet, over the precise wireframe of Louis XIV's Romain du Roi. Which amounts to a typographic oxymoron: a SINGLE typeface that's simultaneously MANY typefaces and never stops moving.

Naming this shape-shifter is easy enough—just shunt another couple of boxcars onto the end of the night train to arrive at (deep breath) Meta-the-difference-between-the-two-Font, or MTDBT2F4D for short.

Writing in one place inevitably *performs* in another. Here, for example, reflecting on Hofstadter's and Morison's and Groys's various assimilations of the terms "letter" and "spirit" fosters a more robust, compound sense of their allegorical purpose. It produces a cosmopolitan thought. When grappling with ideas in one domain is brought to bear on another, those ideas are more firmly grasped and so more readily utilized somewhere else … towards considering, say, the ways in which relative chauvinism and relative open-mindedness manifest themselves in daily life and work. Or, equally, writing the first small script when learning a new programming language, the sole purpose of which is to generate two words that mark the border between instruction and instance. Swaddled in asterisks and set without a full point, this text always reads:

Hello world

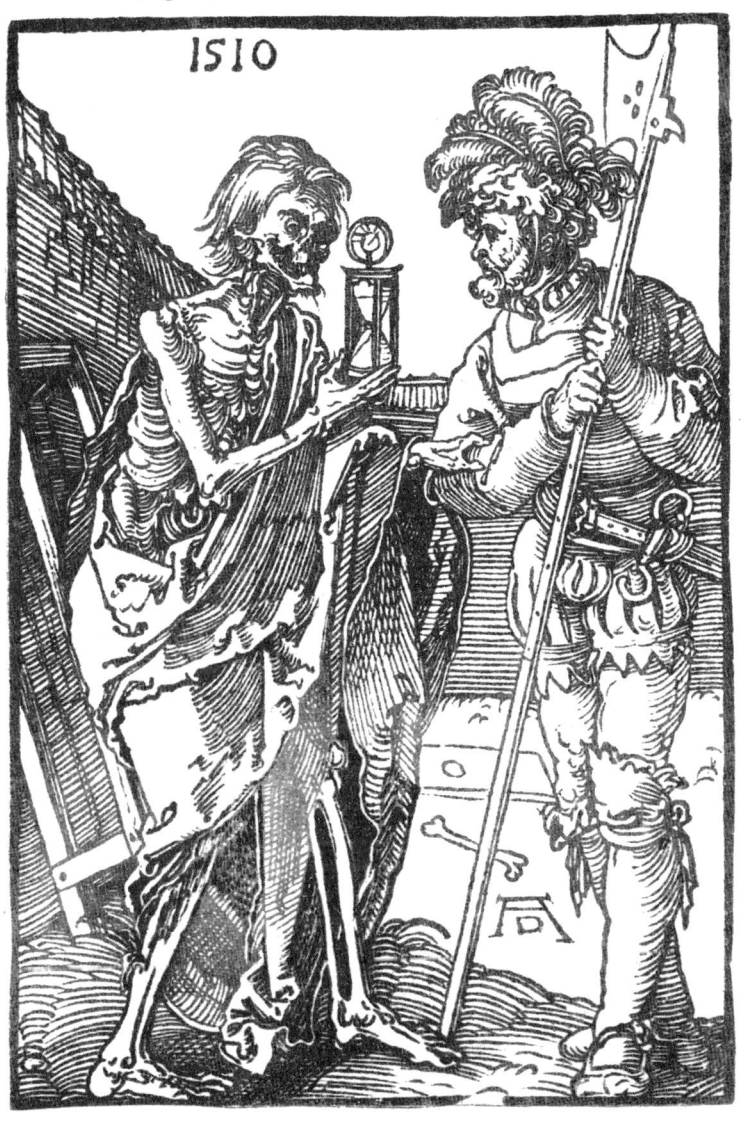

A Note on the Time

The time right now is 2011 Feb 18 3:34:12 PM. But it's not really, is it? At least not for you, right now. Check your phone, your computer, maybe even your watch — certainly it reports something else. What's going on? These two times could never be precisely alike: each is a specific POINT, and no two are ever exactly the same.

The time above — which has in fact been automatically stamped by a custom script embedded in this document — originates from a networked time server maintained by Apple and named, simply, time.apple.com. This external beacon commands not only the official time here on this MacBook, but also synchronizes its local clock with those of Apple users worldwide (laptops, desktops, phones, pods, pads, who-knows-what's-nexts). It's easy enough to think of time.apple.com as a master clock, but actually it is itself only a network of time machines, a collection of counters comprised of a circuit of servers — computers called time1.apple.com, time2.apple.com, time3, time4, time5, time6 and time7. (The server this laptop is using right now (time4) is located at 20400 Stevens Creek Blvd. in Cupertino, California, just a few blocks away from Apple's appropriate corporate address, 1 Infinite Loop.)

All of these servers communicate and agree what time it is at time.apple.com. But this covers only North and South America, and also must synchronize itself with time.asia.apple.com and time.europe.apple.com to provide a truly unified answer. All this close coordination, communicated over distance and time, is governed by Network Time Protocol (NTP), a set of time-sharing conventions developed in advance of the World Wide Web in 1985, by University of Delaware professor Dr. David Mills. It is one of the oldest, and most essential, Internet protocols.

NTP runs as a Ponzi scheme. Each layer in the scheme organizes a set of time servers, who both receive the correct time from the layer above (each layer is properly called a "stratum" in the protocol) and also are responsible for dispersing the correct time to computers in the next layer down. At each level, more and more computers are connected.

The protocol works by sending a message between two points on a network containing two bits of information: (1) What time it is now at the source, and (2) How long it took to transmit this message to its receiver. Simple addition tells you what time it is on the receiving computer (according to the sender). So, what time is it, precisely? Multiply this transaction through the layer cake of millions of computers redundantly organized around the Network Time Protocol, and you'll begin to see a collective consensus emerge that passes for accuracy.

Turns out that in order to send a message between two POINTS, it's essential that the two points AGREE on what time it is, otherwise the communication is jumbled. A quick thought gymnastic confirms. You live in Los Angeles and I live in New York. Settling on Eastern Standard Time, your clock tells you it is 2:34 PM, and mine tells me it is 2:32 PM, and you tell me, "Hey! In one minute the eclipse is going to start, you'd better run outside right now to see it (don't forget your sunglasses)!" and I drop what I'm doing to rush right outside. I see nothing. I'm bummed. I write back, "Nothing doing out there, I must've missed it." You reply, "But the eclipse is scheduled for 2:33 pm! You probably came in too early!" And I respond, "I'd already missed it then. It's 2:34 now." "No you haven't, it's in one minute still!" In the midst of this tedious exchange, surely the moon has passed in front of the sun and everyone in question has missed the party. What a misunderstanding!

These kinds of missteps multiply exponentially over a network, and it should be blindingly clear how critical agreement on the correct time is now, in our intimately connected present.

For communication, then, perhaps time is more of a medium than a measure. If we are going to be able to say anything to each other, we'd better start by agreeing on what time it is.

In the spring of 2012, we were in the middle of designing a rather more primitive time-keeping device. We had been invited to participate in "Nuit Blanche" (White Night), a single evening of art installations in Toronto, open for a mass audience from sunset to sunrise. Perversely, we proposed to install a permanent (and temporarily dysfunctional) sundial. Here is an e-mail from the curator at the time confirming the public language around our project:

Date: Wed, 28 Mar 2012 15:56:13 -0700
Subject: "Nuit Blanche" marketing texts
Hi David and Stuart,

Below is the blurb I've written for the "Nuit Blanche" marketing materials along with one of the images you sent. Please let me know what you think. I'm already past the deadline on this so I'd appreciate your response ASAP:

"Conceived against the grain of "Nuit Blanche," Dexter Sinister's *White Night* is a simple sundial which will be permanently installed and so remain long after the fleeting one-night festival, continually telling time as an ancient expression of civic function. For the duration of Nuit Blanche itself, however, *White Night* will be illuminated from above by powerful klieg lights — a deliberately overblown spectacle designed to render the object curiously functionless on its inaugural night. The simple sundial will be accompanied by a complex caption, a new iteration of a palimpsest text titled 'Notes on the Type & Time.' This essay recounts the history of MetaFont, a math-based typeface originally proposed in the 1970s, then demonstrates a successor by Dexter Sinister called Meta-the-difference-between-the-two-Font, which will be used to typeset the sundial's numerals in brass."

Many thanks,
Christina

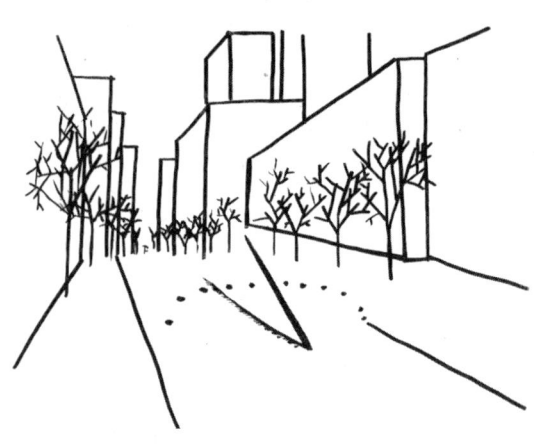

1 2 3 4 5 6 7 8 9 10 11 12

We continued to develop the project until, two weeks before installation, it was suddenly cancelled by the city government and host institution for "political" reasons that were never made entirely clear. That was more than five years ago now.

OK, let's back up for a minute and look again at the time reported in the first sentence of this text. This time was handed down through the cascade of networked time servers described earlier, but where did the original "time" come from and how was it set?

In the top tier of the Network Time Protocol, one computer is hooked directly to one extraordinarily accurate clock. Currently, this is the Cesium Fountain Atomic Clock running at the National Institutes of Standards and Technology laboratory in Boulder, Colorado, named NIST-F1. Atomic clocks rely on the fuzzed logics of quantum mechanics. As electrons orbit the nucleus of an atom, rather than winding down gradually in energy like a pendulum, they lose energy in discrete chunks, at which point the circling electron jumps down to the next closest orbit producing something like a very very very faint "click." These steps are consistent for any one atom, and this quantity is its resonant frequency. The resonant frequency of the cesium atom, for example, is 9,192,631,770 Hertz (or cycles per second). And in a twist of recursive identity, the NIST has set the official standard for 1 second to be equal to 9,192,631,770 vibrations of the cesium atom. The United States' primary time and frequency standard is set then by NIST-F1 and is accurate to within one second every 60 million years.

So you can now more or less assume that the time stamped in the first line of this text does rather accurately reflect when the first sentence was written.

We'd all agree that 2011 Feb 18 3:34:12 PM identifies one specific POINT in time, a forever unrepeatable instant that disappears as quickly as the software can stamp it. 18th-century empirical philosopher David Hume would certainly concur. Working from the center of the Scottish Enlightenment, Hume described his particular, uncompromised version of empiricism. He asserted that everything we know or can know about the world arrives to us only through direct sensory experience. Nothing exists outside of our own practical encounter with it as we move through the world. Further, he suggests that any sensible experience is composed of a single indivisible sensory building block which is marked by the limits of our perception. If you can't experience it, it doesn't exist. Hume most certainly was an essentialist.

While American empirical philosopher William James built many of his ideas on Hume's scaffolds, he also rejected Hume's reductive essentialism. In James's second-wave or "radical" empiricism, although knowledge about the world still arrived through direct experience, he dismissed what he called Hume's "atomism" or the idea that this experience was ever-assembled from smaller elementary blocks. James was, instead, a "Gestaltist"—a totalist who, although insisting on the incrementalism of building the world piece by piece, also understood that any one experience was whole and complete in and of itself, neither equivalent to nor reducible into any constituent bits.

So if we could query Hume about our time marked in the first line of this text, he would identify it as a single irreducible moment. However, ask William James and he says that this POINT is really more of a DURATION. Time is like that—both point *and* duration. This is how it can bend and warp. A week, a second, a season: all are specific and discrete, but none are the same. The present can be cut to any number of lengths, from a single vibration of a cesium atom to the gestation period of a latent sundial project.

By 2016, we were trying to revive the sundial for a situation where it seemed, if nothing else, timely. "The Contemporary Contemporary" is a conference organized at the ARoS Aarhus Art Museum, Denmark, to be held June 16–18, 2017, in the middle of this year's Aarhus Triennial, titled "The Garden: Past, Present, Future." We described and proposed our revived project in an e-mail to the organizers:

> Date: Mon, 31 Oct 2016 12:22:16 +0000
> Subject: Sundial
> Geoff, Jacob,
>
> Following our recent conversations, here's a more involved account of our sundial to use in your upcoming Aarhus Triennial and related conference meetings.
>
> As mentioned, the sundial is a hangover from a previous proposal. However, we don't consider this a mere recycling of something that failed to happen elsewhere; rather, it seems just as appropriate for the "Contemporary Contemporary" context—if not more so.
>
> For obvious reasons, the idea of our installing a sundial chimes with a Triennial founded on the past, present, and future of civic gardens. We want to combine the primitive yet still eminently efficient technology of the sundial with some contemporary elements, such as our Meta-the-difference-between-the-two-Font—a typeface which in a few respects is very *now.*

Our sundial was originally intended to be installed on the campus of the University of Toronto on the occasion of "Nuit Blanche," one of those annual through-the-night art festivals. Although intended as a permanent fixture, it was to be inaugurated on the night by four giant spotlights positioned to illuminate the clock but cast no shadow and so render it spectacularly useless, as a kind of Zero Hour (or 12 hours…) until sunrise when it would begin its first daily cycle. The dial's numbers were to be typeset in a metal version of MTDBT2F, and the plan was to publish some related writing in a modest booklet intended to highlight the various pasts, presents, and futures at play in our thinking about and around the work. This would have been made available in proximity of the dial, to serve as a extended caption of sorts.

Similarly in Aarhus, then, our proposition is to install a hopefully permanent sundial in an appropriate public site — ideally a civic garden. The form of the dial is again about as minimal as it gets: a set of numbers set in a bespoke version of MTDBT2F. We have no particular material in mind for these characters — maybe iron, brass, copper, or some other weatherproof metal native to the region. The Toronto dial was due to be some 3–4 meters in diameter, but there's no particular reason for it to be one size rather another as long as it works, so that's best decided once we settle on a site. It's important to note, though, that in Canada we were working with an expert to determine the precise positioning of the numbers on the ground, along with the length and angle of the pole (or to use the technical term, "gnomon"). Naturally these factors depend on the site's location relative to the sun: the numerals aren't simply distributed evenly around a perfect circle, but rather their spacing depends on local longitude and latitude; and so we'll have to find someone able to crunch the numbers for the Aarhus iteration.

This would be also a great opportunity to announce and release our book in The Contemporary Condition series. We imagine this comprising two related essays about MTDBT2F, along with a third that charts the social ambiguity and technological standardization of our contemporary sense of time. All three are elastic, designed to be transformed each time they're published. In the first essay "A Note on the Type," for instance, we demonstrate what happens when the font's meta-level parameters are changed by typesetting excerpts from other people's writing in wildly different versions; and while the essay's generic template always remains the same, these excerpts are chosen to speak to the particular context of publication. Its sister essay "A Note on the Time" is similarly palimpsestuous in that we've previously rewritten the ending in a few different ways — to turn it into a ten-year font license for Kadist Art Foundation, for instance. And so we can readily imagine reworking this last essay in view of proposing a sundial for Aarhus; or if that pitch doesn't work, anywhere else in the world.

As in Toronto, the sundial and the book are conceived as constituent parts of the overall work, perhaps along with a plaque in the vicinity of the dial that tethers them. But for Aarhus we further propose a new, third component; some kind of digital incarnation of the emphatically analogue sundial. So far as we've (barely) thought this through, we imagine running a clock from an online server that generates a live virtual sundial graphic based on the location of the viewer's hardware — just like a physical one. Consider this a server- rather than a sundial, rendering a slowly-turning pixel-black shadow in real-time based on the viewer's coordinates. This could be channeled via a single webpage or as part of a more complex site, but we can also imagine projecting an up-scaled public version high on a wall during the conference.

What might it mean to literally *project a shadow,*
meaning one made by the negative light of a video
projector? Whatever the answer, we suspect it might well
resonate with the broader themes of your "Contemporary
Condition" research project.

Regards,

DS

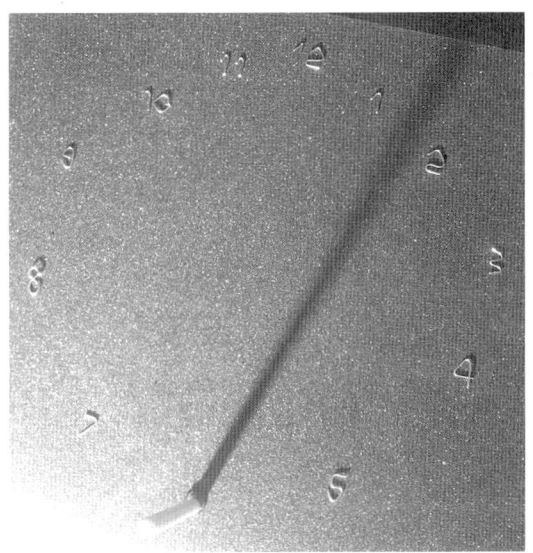

This e-mail was sent 2016 Oct 31 12:22:16 PM. At the time
of writing, the possibility of realizing the sundial in Aarhus
remains unresolved. In the meantime, we have forged ahead
with its attendant text. You're reading it, now.

So let's flashback one more time to that time stamped
in the first sentence of this essay: 2011 Feb 18 3:34:12 PM.
We'll agree that the difference between these two points
describes a length, but how can we measure it? Our meter-
stick won't do. Time is nothing until it is counted, and for that
we need a clock.

In *From Sundials to Atomic Clocks: Understanding Time and Frequency*, James Jespersen and Jane Fitz-Randolph describe keeping time as only a matter of counting the ticks of any regular, cyclical action. They also describe the constituent parts of a "clock" (or more properly a "clock system"). Schematically, it looks like this:

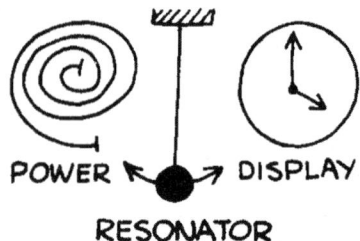

First, you need a device that can produce a periodic pheno-menon (for example, a pendulum). This is the RESONATOR. Next you'll have to sustain the periodic motion by feeding it POWER (for example, the wound coil of a mechanical clock spring). Finally you need a means for counting, accumulating and rendering the ticks of the resonator. This is the DISPLAY (for example, a clock face and hands). Together, these three pieces define a clock. But of course to be useful—to measure a length—our clock must be RUNNING. With all of these conditions met, we can now simply determine the duration between writing the first sentence of this text and editing this one: 2285 days, 17 hours, 25 minutes, 48 seconds. And this delivers one final paradox: Time can only be measured by MOVING.

Date: Wed, 7 Dec 2016 12:49:00 +0000
Subject: Serverdial
Geoff, Jacob,
Here's our current thinking about and around our contribution to the Aarhus conference. Above all, we're still very much committed to making an actual physical sundial,

even if that now seems impossible in the context of the Triennial due to the usual shortfalls of time and money. It's important for us to keep in mind that any virtual version is always relative to an equivalent one on the ground; but we're happy enough to reverse engineer the idea here and effectively do the second thing first.

To recap, the idea is to program some kind of digital sundial, or serverdial, to be projected at the "Contemporary Contemporary" conference next June. In advance of this *installed virtual* version we also propose to make a placeholder rendering — an artists' impression — that you could perhaps use to publicize the entire conference. Visually speaking, it will be extremely rudimentary: some play of positive light and its inverse shade that turns on the logic of a sun-based clock. Yet behind this simple surface would lie a far more complex system that takes into account the local geographic coordinates of Aarhus, the angle of the sun according to the season and time of day relative to the city's position on the globe. (Auspiciously enough, we've just realized that this digi-dial shares many characteristics with that cartoon contemporary Apple "throbber" icon incorporated into our design for the "Contemporary Condition" series, moving through 12 shades of grey over as many books.)

For now the idea is based on these principles:

1. The URL serverdial.org is a live 3-D working clock interface with two key elements: the spacing of the numbers, and the angle of the gnomon, both of which automagically adjust relative to where you are in the world. As such, it *serves* as a tool for designing and implementing any future sundial at any specific location — in view of, but not limited to, Aarhus, for example.

2. The server supplants the sun. Time is provided by de facto Network Time Protocol, which means that the pixels on the screen are a live index of the NTP protocol in

action, just as the shadow on the ground is a live index of the sun's movements.

3. The serverdial has a two-fold application. On one hand, it is a TOOL for digitally modeling a physical sundial—though you have to go to the actual site of your future sundial for the software model to be accurate. On the other hand, it's a working DEVICE for displaying the current time—though it only works on a smartphone laid horizontal, otherwise its X, Y, and Z axes are mixed up in gyroscopic, hyperbolic space.

For now we're sending along this image of the interface-in-progress, being a current model based on a previous proposal in advance of its pending realization. You might think of it as a shadow of its future self.

More soon,
DS

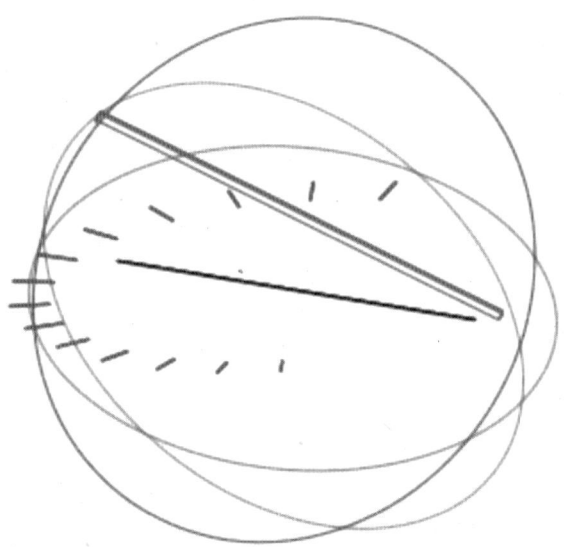

http://www.serverdial.org

GENEALOGY

"A Note on the Type" was first published in *The Curse of Bigness* to accompany an exhibition of the same name at Queens Museum of Art (2010), then — variously reworked and incorporating new "sample" excerpts — as a wall vinyl that comprised an exhibition called "The Plastic Arts," Gallery 400 at University of Illinois, Chicago (2010); as a text in the journal *Dot Dot Dot* #20 (2010); in vinyl again for the exhibitions "A Note on the Signs" at Artissima, Turin (2010), and "A Note on the T" at Graphic Design Worlds, Milan (2011); as a text in the journals *Bulletins of The Serving Library* #1 (2011) and *Afterall* 27 (2011), magazine *Art in America* (2013), the book *Graphic Design: History in the Making* (Occasional Papers, 2017), and in a form combined with its sequel "Letter & Spirit" in *Simplicity: Ideals of Practice in Mathematics and the Arts* (Springer, 2017).

"Letter & Spirit" was first published in *Bulletins of The Serving Library* #3 (2012), then — in an animated form first used to render a "Trailer for the Exhibition Catalog" in the show *Ecstatic Alphabets/ Heaps of Language* at Museum of Modern Art, New York (2012) — variously distilled into a "film" of live code screened at the Festival de l'Affiche Chaumont (2012), Tramway, Glasgow (2012), CCA Glasgow (2012), and Charlottenborg, Copenhagen (2012); then as a part of two Dexter Sinister solo exhibitions, *Work-in-Progress*, CAC Vilnius (2014), and *On a Universal Serial Bus**, Kunstverein München, Munich (2015) — the latter alongside parallel publication of the text in the show's "Companion" book *On a Universal Serial Bus** (ROMA/Kunstverein München, 2015), and a compilation of audio-visual works on the flash drive *Universal Serial Bus* (Sternberg Press, 2015); and in a form combined with its prequel "Letter & Spirit" in *Simplicity: Ideals of Practice in Mathematics and the Arts* (Springer, 2017).

"A Note on the Time" was first published in *Bulletins of The Serving Library* #1 (2011), then variously retooled for *Art Journal* (2011); a bilingual pamphlet in English and Italian, printed on the occasion of Alighiero e Boetti Day, Turin (2011); as part of a larger PDF publication released alongside the exhibition "Counter-Production," Generali Foundation, Vienna (2012); transfigured into the "instruc-tions" for Watch Wyoscan 0.5 Hz, a reverse-engineered Casio digital watch produced by Halmos with additional support from Objectif Editions, Antwerp, and Yale Union, Portland, OR (2012); collected in *Time*, from the Whitechapel: Documents of Contemporary Art series (MIT Press, 2013); and finally retooled with the other two essays to serve as a font license and style guide for Kadist Art Foundation (2014), which was the immediate forerunner of the present volume.

Dexter Sinister is the compound name of Stuart Bertolotti-Bailey and David Reinfurt, who operate at the intersection of graphic design, publishing, and contemporary art. In 2006, Dexter Sinister established a workshop and bookstore of the same name in New York, and have since explored aspects of contemporary publishing in diverse contexts. As well as designing, editing, producing, and distributing both printed and digital media, they have also worked with ambiguous roles and formats, usually in the live contexts of galleries and museums. These projects generally play to some form of site-specificity, where a publication or series of events are worked out in public over a set period of time.

Their writing and other work is available in the Dexter Sinister publications *Portable Document Format* (Berlin: Sternberg Press, 2009), *Universal Serial Bus* (Berlin: Sternberg Press, 2015), and *On a Universal Serial Bus** (Amsterdam: ROMA; Munich: Kunstverein München, 2015). They have also published frequently via *Dot Dot Dot*, a left-field arts journal that Bertolotti-Bailey cofounded and initially coedited with Peter Bilak in 2000, then later together with Reinfurt from 2006 to 2010; as well as its successor *Bulletins of The Serving Library*, together with Francesca Bertolotti-Bailey and Angie Keefer since 2011.

They are currently working on a modular audio-visual project called *The Last ShOt Clock* that considers ways and means of exiting regular modes of time.

The Contemporary Condition book series offers a sustained inquiry into the contemporary condition from a range of perspectives by key commentators who investigate contemporaneity as a defining condition of our historical present. Contemporaneity refers to the temporal complexity that follows from the coming together in the same cultural space of heterogeneous clusters generated along different historical trajectories, across different scales, and in different localities. With the overall aim of questioning the formation of subjectivity in time and the concept of temporality in the world now, it is a basic assumption that art can operate as an advanced laboratory for investigating processes of meaning-making and for understanding wider developments within culture and society. The series identifies three broad lines of inquiry for investigation: the issue of temporality, the role of contemporary media and computational technologies, and how artistic practice makes epistemic claims.

Sternberg Press